Eva, My Nani-Ji

Written by: Djamil Ninsoo

Copyright

Eva, My Nani-Ji by Djamil Ninsoo

Copyright © 2022 Djamil Ninsoo

ISBN: 9798450009964

Dedicated to Eva L. Williams, my amazing Nani-Ji from Richmond Road, whose love and guidance has made me the man I am today.

To my future children, may you learn and draw inspiration from your Par-Aji.

There is a lush green island in the sun, surrounded by the bright blue waters of the Caribbean Sea called Jamaica.
And on this island, there is an old *dougla* woman.
You will find her sitting on her veranda, looking out on the world around her.
Admiring the doctor birds as they flit amongst the bougainvillea growing on the wall.
Her hair, silver and curly.
Soft and welcoming, her smile.

She wasn't always old though.
Oh no, long before the **kiangkro** left its marks along her
cheery cheeks and age began to cast its shroud over her
bright brown eyes. Before she became the matriarch of a
dynasty stretching five lifetimes
The old **dougla** woman regales to me the story
of when she was
the young **dougla** girl.

Born on the 24th day of April 1939, the little *dougla* baby named Lovina Anderson filled her little home in Richmond Road, Saint Mary with excitement. Much to the joy of her anxiously awaiting parents William Anderson and Alice Nelson. The long-awaited daughter was happily welcomed by her loving older brothers Kenneth, George, Clifford, and Percell.

The young *dougla* girl grew up fast, but she always made time for her *Nana* Ninsoo. He had come across the *kala pani*, *a jahaji* from Mother India, many years ago to work on plantations tending banana and cocoa. Though his face escapes her memory, she recalls him wearing his white Indian wrapper, never lighting his kitchen fire till Friday *namaz* were made. Sharing with her: sada roti, *baigan choka*, and *gulgula*.

The granddaughter of Indenture and Slavery, the young *dougla* girl loudly and proudly celebrates her festivals. The frightening, yet amusing costumes of *Junkunu* in the winter. The kaleidoscope of towering *tazias* and rhythmic tassa drums on *Hoosay* in the summer. Just two of her many holidays throughout the year.

Always the adventurer, the young *dougla* girl would cross the river of Cuffy Gully five times on her journey. Far up in the hills, on land her *Nana* Ninsoo gave her mother Alice, was a pen filled with squealing pigs. The young *dougla* girl always made sure to bring food like mashed breadfruit, apples, banana, and corn to feed their hungry snouts.

One November night in 1953, when she was only fourteen years old the young *dougla* girl received word that her *Mausi* Margaret was in hospital and needed to be brought home. Tagging behind her father, the young *dougla* girl loaded up in a borrowed truck from and set out for Annotto Bay. Unfortunately, on the way to the hospital the truck broke down. This did not stop the travelers however, as a dedicated few led by the young *dougla* girl made the rest of the journey on foot.

It was 29 Apr. 1959 in Saint Ann when the young *dougla* girl became the blushing *dougla* bride of Mr. Ivanhoe Williams, of Highgate, just five days after her 20th birthday. The blushing *dougla* bride looked like a princess out of a fairytale, in her dress of white made of lace and tulle, holding her bouquet of stephanotis and orchids. Her bright smile as wide as her handsome groom is tall.

As the newlywed couple leaves the old Bethlehem Gospel Hall Church, the blushing *dougla* bride sheds tears as she prepares to leave behind not just her parents and brothers, but her *Mausi* Sarah, *Mamu* Alex, cousins Betty, Nanku, and many others; however, she knows no matter how far she goes and no matter what comes, family will always remain. So, she smiles as she thinks about what her future holds.

A future full of life, laughter, and love as the young
dougla bride becomes a:
Wife,
Mother,
Aunt,
Grandmother,
Great-Grandmother,
Great-Great Grandmother,
Matriarch,
Friend,
Mentor,
Counsellor.
But no matter the role
she will always be
Eva Lovina Williams,
My Nani-Ji.

Glossary

Baigan Choka - Indian roast eggplant dish (Caribbean Hindustani).

Dougla - Afro-East Indian mixed race (Caribbean Hindustani).

Gulgula - Indian fried banana fritter (Caribbean Hindustani).

Hoosay - Muslim Indo-Caribbean observance. (Caribbean Hindustani).

Jahaji – Indentured Labourer from India (Caribbean Hindustani)

Junkunu - African street parade. (Jamaican Patois).

Kala Pani – Dark waters, Ocean (Caribbean Hindustani).

Kiangkro - Vulture (Jamaican Patois).

Mamu - Maternal uncle (Caribbean Hindustani).

Mausi - Maternal aunt (Caribbean Hindustani).

Nana - Maternal grandfather (Caribbean Hindustani).

Nani - Maternal grandmother (Caribbean Hindustani).

Namaz – Prayer (Caribbean Hindustani)

Tazia - Structure built during Hoosay. (Caribbean Hindustani).

Made in United States
Orlando, FL
06 July 2024